Gospel Road Going

Gospel Road Going

poems

Michael Chitwood

TRYON PUBLISHING COMPANY, INC.
CHAPEL HILL

ACKNOWLEDGMENTS

Acknowledgments and thanks are given to the editors and readers of the following magazines in which these poems first appeared:

Blackbird: "The Saved," "Dollar Bill"
Chattahoochee Review: "Those Dying Generations"
Field: "Past Due"
Meridian: "Heat"
Mossy Creek Reader: "Their Telephones," "Their Potatoes," "Their Whatnots," "Their Lakes," "Their Caskets," "Their Dances"
North Carolina Literary Review: "In Country Graveyards," "The Laugh"
Now & Then: "Learning Curve"
Oxford American: "The Donated Organ"
Poetry: "Transport in Early Spring"
Shenandoah: "Sunday Supper"
South Carolina Review: "Woodpile"
Southern Cultures: "The Great Wagon Road…"
The Southern Review: "Sumac"
The Sun: "Afterlife"
Tar River Poetry: "To Be Written Down First Thing in the Morning"
Threepenny Review: "All Saints' Eve"
Virginia Quarterly Review: "The Body," "Sunday Supper"

Printed in the United States of America
Published by
Tryon Publishing Company, Inc.
P.O. Box 1138
Chapel Hill, North Carolina

Cover & Book Design by
Julia Calhoun Williams

First Edition
First Printing

ISBN 1-884824-32-3

for The Mountain Boys,
Michael McFee and Gary Bolt

TABLE OF CONTENTS

I

THE GREAT WAGON ROAD, or
WHY APPALACHIANS ARE MOUNTAINS
AND A PEOPLE

Scottish, by way of Ulster, Philadelphia,
the Valley of the Shenandoah,

generous, clannish, violent, kind-hearted,
they walked in (the Germans rode)

and stayed mostly out of county records
and the backs of Bibles, unlettered.

Their only correspondence with me,
son of their children's children's great grandchildren,

is this ditch, these nearly healed wheel cuts,
the line they traced in the earth.

                          *

Locally, it took its name from where it was going,
the potent away-from-here, the better place,

the how-it-could-be, not wintering on beans,
the infant not dead with the flux,

the ground not snagged with roots
that sang from the plow's cut and welted the shins.

Yonder. Chewed with scratch biscuits,
smoked in the porch shade,

something to be believed
when believing was the only solace.

                          *

"Fortunately, only Single Brothers
made this trip. This trail

at times is impassable and these folk
are wild, unpredictable.

Unlike our brethren,
they came not seeking but fleeing,

the almshouse, the sheriff,
a shamed woman or her brothers.

We sought the freedom to worship.
They worshipped freedom from seeking."

*

"I don't know now, though I knew...."
Her palsied hand goes to her forehead

as if to draw memory with a touch.
My past grows dim,

illiterate, abandoned,
free for the taking.

*

A boy of eight, he killed
one of the King's overlords

for casting a desirous eye on his mother,
and stowed away to sail the whale road.

Saving the crew and cargo from storm,
he was rewarded in Philadelphia

with a seventeen-hand stallion
and rode out of the city stench

to the Blue Ridge which reminded him of home.
There he killed and married Cherokee,

fathered seven sons and seven daughters,
coaxed Highland pipes from fiddle's catgut,

distilled moonlight, slaughtered hogs,
lost fingers in sawmills,

hoed, suckered, topped and primed tobacco,
discarded washing machines in creekbeds,

learned to read the Bible, believe obituaries
and recite where he was and what he was doing

when the first Ford, radio, television
and news of JFK's death arrived.

He put on a tie, conditioned the air
and forgot the song of the whippoorwill.

                         *

"There is no history, but histories."
His shoes aren't right for this rough ground.

The sapling branches whip his back
as he backs into where we're going.

Educated, tenured, he hopes to publish
a study of The Great Wagon Road.

"Until documented the facts are in flux."
He is lecturing backward into the understory

where a honeysuckle vine catches his heel.
He barks his bald spot on a sweet gum

and is silenced into the fact of himself.
Out cold, he's received his dissertation's introduction.

                    *

Count Casimir Pulaski, Bishop
Francis Asbury, Lorenzo Dow,

the Moravian Single Brother who wrote
"We had to watch our horses closely...."

They crossed Maggodee, Blackwater,
and Pigg, scribbled down some thoughts

that I'm stealing outright,
keeping an eye on their horses, too.

Warrior's Trace, gospel road, going now
into sumac, scrub pine and books.

I take your dirt in my hand.
I take your dirt in my hand and move on.

II

Their Spectacles

were swiped with shirttail
or hemline, pushed back
to proper seating with the back
of the hand when they slid
on sweat from canning's roil
or rasping saw.
Here, have a look
through a gone man's glasses.
Our eyes have now nearly adjusted
to fit these prescriptions
found in the back of a drawer.

Their Telephones

were black as Bibles with a luckless
spell wheel of numeral and alphabet.
Holy trinities of vowel and consonant
were rubbed round the dial
for the prayer chain, a sickness
or a hardship passed earpiece,
through the scaly claws of starlings,
to earpiece. The one thick antler,
knobbed as though nurtured on acorns,
how they lifted it to sound the call.

Their Whatnots

caught dust on the whatnot shelf,
nicknack shrine to travel,
glass alligator "Souvenir of Crystal Springs,"
collectable for having gone,
gimcracks of other places,
ward-offs and incants
against having to live there.

Their Potatoes

needed just one eye, needed
a prayer said over them, grease,
a paper bag to soak translucent as a stained-
glass window depicting the Crucifixion,
some meat, a cool, dim place
to grow spikes,
prongs, thorny racks and sleek tusks,
bucks and bristly boars
that gored the dark to live.

Their Dances

were like construction,
hammering heels and music made of wire.
They held the torso plumb and still
enough for a church pew,
but below the waist all Hell
broke lose in jigs
on the little plyboard squares
they threw down in a pasture
to build the palaces of joy.

Their Caskets

were good furniture, saved for
or borrowed for, sheen,
brass, buffed and upholstered
such as divans never had been.
This one time they could afford
the best, this rest
would cost the living pretty.

Their Radios

etched in the outside world,
staticky status
for those who could afford them,
nearly big as a closet,
certainly big enough for burying a baby
as they would all their children,
going out to what was coming in.

Their Lakes

have fish and houses in them,
the drowned, the old homeplace, a '58 Ford,
angels with Evinrudes and crank bait
above those farms and low-rent shacks
the power company left standing in the depths.
The air of those front yards is tannic,
silty, scale-spangled and slick with dark.
It would kill us to live there.

III

Those Dying Generations

I. The End of the World, At Least for Today

That would have been in March
of the year Elaine was born in January
was how she remembered
and created my past's past,
begetting me, all of us, out of the daily,
as though every event was a tit for tat,
this happened because of that
which is how I might remember a happiness
in the year that blank space
that's unbalanced my grandfather's stone,
he for years with two dates, her with one,
is filled in
as the earth will be beside him.
What will be forgotten I hope
are these afternoons, these long evenings,
unable to remember the names
of children, no one answering the bell,
not this for not that,
the nothing that happens
for so long each night.

II. Attendant

This is the past's warehouse.
The past gags youngsters
coming into its fumes of urine
and regurgitated saltless meals.
You get used to it if you work here.
You hardly hear the moans and shouts,
those calls for husbands, mothers, fathers,
thirty years dead but again alive
and leaving the ones who shout alone
where they can't get out of bed
and they are being robbed of money,
dresses, the bread we baked for the preacher,

the preacher who married our daughter
and took her off to Iowa one winter
where she froze, oh he killed her,
as they are killing us with rays
from the TV, with what they put in the food,
with those blue booties cutting off
our circulation, our feet, our breath.
Us. Them. Our. Are they here yet?
The dead make regular visits.
You get used to it if you work here.
These are the ones who churned butter,
and primed tobacco and made dresses
out of feed sacks and killed hogs,
ah God I hate when they kill hogs,
the smack of the flat side of the ax,
the scalding, the scraping,
working the meat, shoulders, hams,
liver and lights, the brains, cleaning
the intestines, the intestines!
And they complain about what
we bring them to eat.
We killed day after Thanksgiving.
We killed first full moon after the frost.
We killed when the persimmons ripened.
Damn that past with its happy butchers.

But this is the last of them,
last of those ones who did without,
last of the ones who hate having
anything done for them.
This is the last of the ones
that knife you with their eyes
when you help them, clean them,
keep them alive another day.
Bed-bound, burning with memory,
they know you as sister, brother,
son, daughter, one of them.
They think I should know better
than to help them, feed them.
They hate the living I earn
at their living's expense
and you can't get used to that.

III. The Cure

It's taken eighty-eight years to get her body
so that it will lie here
beneath this blanket while a story spills out
in whispers or maybe just sighs,
the stitchery of her thousand veins visible,
the workmanship showing
in her cheeks, her arms, even her fingers,
every visible piece of skin.
No grease; no fatback; no salt here,
the bendable straw cocked to her mouth
like a microphone, the oxygen snout above her head ready,
the call button on its cord dangling within reach.
"They don't come when I call"
and we come when we can, called by eighty-eight years of her,
the one famous to us for our lives,
and the stories of our lives,
draining out of her tethered to the IV,
to the medication, to the physical therapist, the psychotherapist,
the dietitian, the physician, the x-ray technician,
it was Uncle Jim Bennett was called
because I had gotten the erysipelas
from a bob wire scratch
and Dr. Gale had come with some black grease
but my leg still burned
and Uncle Jim Bennett says there could be nobody in the house,
save us, and I could not look
but what I felt was him breathing on the leg,
it could have been some words he said.
He came back every hour for three hours
and I walked the next day therapist, the dietitian, the
psychotherapist, the physical therapist, the
chaplain, the social worker, the radiologist *one of them,*
it might have been Nancy, had the thrush,
broke out all around her mouth and could barely eat.
Somebody, it might have been Papa ET,
sent for Sis Angle
and she cupped her hand around the baby's mouth
and blew out the thrush.

Say what you will
a baby don't know to get better but did.
This spook talk amuses, puzzles,
is a manifestation, a symptom, a way of self-grieving,
nonsense mumbling to the physician, nurse, psychotherapist,
physical therapist, chaplain.
It's ignorant or at best unlearned,
accented, these days unheard of,
though never actually heard but felt in the saying.
It has lived this long
and still there are whispers.
Here, right now. Whatever these sighs mean.
They might be words,
the cure in them.

The Body

They clutched pocketbooks in their laps
and crumpled a tissue in one hand.
Their hose were nearly pants,
so thick and brown,
and their shoes laced up,
not like Mom's high heels.

But they were the only ones who touched her
in her shiny walnut bed, the best
piece of furniture she'd ever owned.
Her mouth had its teeth again,
her finger the wedding band
that had rested on the sill above the sink.

It was only the great aunts
who reached in unafraid,
their blue-veined hands
shaking until they touched hers
and then they were still together.
Steadied, they said the nothing there was to say,
but lingered by the body the years had made
nearly identical to their own.

To Be Written Down First Thing in the Morning

And then I see her
coming from the basement,
a whiff of that damp room's musk comes with her,
and she is carrying
one of those old fashioned, clamp-on contraptions
for peeling apples.
She has it by its stout brass base
and the chiming blade sets ring with her steps.
The wooden handle of the crank has a lacquered sheen
from years of hands.
You jammed the fruit onto those two thin prongs
and turned the crank to work the blades.
Peel came off like cursive sentences,
fragrant, long statements the hogs loved.
It was a marvel in 1932,
and look at her, young again,
after just three years with death,
holding out this brass, jingling wonder like a candelabra.
She lifts it for me to see.
This is happiness.
Soon she'll have it going.

The Laugh

I think of him wreathed in smoke,
match just blown out with a puff of his visible death,
his ghost breath from the Lucky Strike.

He flicks a greeting, lifting his index nub
(a table saw took its tip) from the steering wheel,
and the brass catches of his bibs click

as he chuckles with memory,
recalls a time that he and the father
of "the fellow we just passed

went down to the river on a Saturday night
to see what, besides mosquitoes, was biting.
We'd barely gotten a line wet

when, without even the warning of a cigarette tip,
the warden asks from the dark bank top
for a license from each of us.

Well, I split the river and the warden
right after me, up the opposite bank
and through Ned Hudson's cane field

laying down cane like a mower would.
One hand on a fence post and I was over
and heard a barb rip the county man's cloth.

Halfway to the paved road,
I gave the warden some ease,
saying I always had to run

when one of those cramps hit me,
he knew how that was didn't he?
I showed him my license, purple ink still fresh.

And the other fellow who worried all day
that his mill check hadn't bought a fishing stamp,
well, he was back of his woodshed by then,

cleaning the catfish our splashing spooked
to his bait...."
Here coughing and laughter fought

for his breath and he tapped the wheel
with the heel of his palm.
He'd never forget the warden's look.

I have not forgotten his not forgetting
or how the smoke of his laugh ribboned around us
and vanished out the lowered window.

In Country Graveyards

Several month's wages
went into the adult monuments,
some big as a bed's headboard
where a couple, he on the right,
she on the left, just as in life,
share their final slumber.

These were the anticipated,
the almost looked forward to,
in some cases prayed for,
and paid for in advance.

But close by the older ones
are one or two creekstones,
narrow end jabbed in the turf,
a foot and a half of granite
for the stillborns, sick infants.
No names or dates or scripture quote.
Only gray, water-polished rocks,
just the size of what they mark.

Learning Curve

The weeks were strict, practicing cursive
in the desk Granddad had salvaged.
With the hand-held sander he had erased
curses, initials, couples hitched with a plus

and left a slick surface for my writing tablet.
The exercise pages held county two-lanes,
two solid lines and a broken middle stripe
to help regulate my vowels and consonants.

There began the track of my scrawled record
of unlettered granddaddy and bookless kin,
the elementary roads waiting for my pen's tar,
my looping and circling testament to blood.

Whitewashing the Maples

She's come out on the porch to supervise,
her cane with its three-pronged base
stands beside the scalloped-backed tin chair.

I can see remnants of the last job in crevices.
"It dresses up the yard so," she had pleaded.
"Redneck art," I think as I slap on the stain

of old craft, this, covering what needs no cover,
the berry-stained hand smacked on a dim cave wall.
Look, the tall ladies have pulled on white stockings.

Mudroom

Few houses have them now.
It was where you left the stink of the barn,
oil-stained coat, manure-caked boots.

Usually in a basement,
a shower nozzle in the corner,
a strand of wire to drape the pungent clothes on.

You left work there
and rose into the evening news,
what the world did while you made hay.

Each morning you'd descend,
put on the aromas of your work,
not unpleasant, the WD-40, straw,

the spurt from the grease nipple,
the cuff full of timothy,
the mud you'd wear another day.

Heat

A Coke bottle stopped
with a sprinkle head
sat at one end of the board.
She'd swap iron for bottle,
splash the cloth,
then go at it with the iron.
The crooked was made straight,
the wrinkled smooth,
and she'd lecture from that altar
where rumpled sheets went crisp.
"If Old Scratch gets his claws
in your thigh or neck,
you burn a thousand years
and that is the first day."
Our clothes got rigid,
seam matched seam.
Our bodies would ruin her work.

Afterlife

She taped little labels
to the cast iron skillet,
a bracelet, a pair of scissors.
A confetti of our names
collected on her effects,
a bone-handle razor,
her father's, marked for me.
From the other side
she's saying, "Shave."
"How about a blue pin
with that dress?"
"Bake cornbread in this."
"Here. Take this. Here."

Lament for the Lard Firkin

Lard Firkin. Chain Trace. Thunder Mug.
We don't need these words anymore.

No one said abstract expressionism
when they whitewashed the maples.

The Zenith voice box took up one whole corner
with its façade like a cathedral window.

No one said façade.
No one said cathedral

though they ran a plumb line
and built a Methodist church.

Clapboard. Woodstove. Altar Call.
They dismantled two hogs

to make it through the winter.
Souse Meat. Cracklings. Liver Pudding.

Those too can go.
You don't have to know a treadle

from a two-man saw.
Come butter come

is no way to talk.
Goodbye good words

and the mouths they fit.
We don't need names now

for the gear to get up a mule.
We don't need a wagon tongue,

and saying it
will not make it so.

IV

The Risen

For years of my childhood, the road out
was dirt, not "hard serviced" I thought they said.
And church was services, long and the pews hard,
so I thought I got it.
Anyone leaving or coming to our house
raised a cloud. On the other side
of the road was a cemetery.
Hard not to get metaphorical about this,
but the dust was literal I saw
when they opened a grave,
some distant family calling for a loved one
buried out of place long ago.
The backhoe tried to lift the rotted casket
which crumbled, and there it was, the loved dust.
So the dead really rose and long before the Rapture.
They trailed our Chevrolets.
They swept down across the yard and settled in the pockets
of shirts on the clothesline. Sunday we'd put them on
and go believe in The Resurrection.

The Donated Organ

Its sweet tones were an audible candy.
The lute, the oboe, the trumpet,
a whole orchestra was caught
in its fine-grain cabinet.
All for the glory of God.
There was the modest brass plaque,
no bigger than a playing card,
that identified the donor—
founder, alderman, merchant—
whose fortune was made selling sugar
to the moonshiners
whose busthead trucked north
into cheap drunks
and rooms chronic with sad tunes.

The Saved

From cutting the nuts out of a bull calf's bag with a Barlow,
from laying case knives on a dress pattern,
from running a trot line and baiting the hooks with gone liver,
from mashing a tobacco worm into a green blot,
from crimping dough at the pie crust edge,
from whisking an egg,
from whipping a boy with a switch he fetched,
from doffing a bolt of taffeta,
from working the one arm of the adding machine,
from beating the answers out of the erasers
Oh Lamb of God, they come.

If you
would be
born again,
if you
would purge
your sin
in the scalding
blood, the blood
shed for you,
if you
would accept
the death
into the water
and the life
rising out,
come.

Three stars inside the moon's halo three nights in a row.
When a snapper latches on, he'll only release if it thunders.
Maud Brown could blow thrush from a baby's mouth.
Phillip Amos would take fire out.
Shirleen Anderson could speak warts away.
To bring someone home, take a lock of their hair and walk
backward to their door and in over the threshold.
Lard rendered on the wrong side of the moon will go rancid.

(no break)

47

A pregnant woman should not look at the full moon or even
the full moon's reflection.

He cried out
and asked
his father
why he was
forsaken.
I want you
fathers and
you mothers
to think
on that,
your only child,
nails tearing
his hands,
those hands
you held.
Spikes driven
into those feet
you washed
and kissed
when they
were dry,
think on
this gift
you fathers
and mothers.

Mud randy as a ripe corpse.
River thick brown, a liquid road, going on its own dirt and
taking its path as it goes.
A canopy of green, a living, breathing roof and the light
through it green.
Mockingbirds splash. Amble of the opossum. Cardinal a red
thread run through the green warp.
Moccasin a muscle brown and blunt.
Frog all fart, all *ja-rump*, all slap and not a bad meal
if you have a mess.
Carp nudge a drowned cow and sup.
The green buzz and crawl of it all.

Take His hand.
Come down
this aisle
tonight. Name
Jesus as your
Lord and
Savior.
Hold those
bleeding hands.
He died
that you
might live,
that you
might not
know the Devil's
breath on
your neck,
a breath
like sour milk.
He feeds
on flesh,
the maggoty
flesh of
this world.
He died
that you
would not
feel the Devil's
claws in
your soft skin,
those claws
crusted and brown
with old blood.
I'm holding
the Devil off
right now,
but Old Scratch
wants you.
He wants
you to stay
in your pew.
He wants you

to think about
a new car,
that TV show,
that baseball glove,
that Barbie.
Are you thinking
about them?
If you are,
the Devil's grinning.

Poplar and gum. Some oak and maple. Sassafras and
dogwood in the understory.
Blackberry bramble white in May with blooms that by July will
be fat drops of sweet ink.
Whippoorwills address the evening in our tongue.
And bobwhites the day. Crows laugh. Terrapins hiss.
Squirrels bark and dogs bark and the groundhog whistles a
tune, a tune from roots, a tune fed by timothy and purple
clover, a tune from fur and yellow ever-growing teeth, a tune
from sturdy little hands and their dirt-polished claws, a tune
most local, a sinful tune if this world is sin.

Don't you
see him
grinning?
Don't you
see his sharp
yellow teeth?
Don't you
hear him whistle
that little tune
for dancing
in the sulfurous fires?
Don't you
hear that tune,
that beautiful
little tune,
he whistles
just for you?

Last Night of the Revival

We grow vivid,
like the page

in the photo album
where the color shots

begin. Pink. Red.
Flushed with body

heat and salvation,
God's rash tinting

ears, necks, cheeks,
so many crowded in

and the furnace below
working against

the worldly wind.
"Come in,

O Sinner,
come in."

Going out
we begin

a new life.
The night, snow,

bare oaks, moon,
all black and white.

How would
our bodies,

breathing the tang
of stars,

not love
this cold?

Sunday Supper

Something the preacher said
about tradition,
"the corpse buried facing east,"
has them comparing the High Street cemetery
to our county plot.

We know our kin's bodies won't waken,
but Uncle Ray says
"if they stood up they'd face the rising sun,"
and that settles the question.

Or rather turns it back
to the Thurman woman found dead
"what was her sister's name,
the one, also dead, who married an Overfelt
with the garage below Redwood?"

Tradition is the wander of their talk,
the crooked paths of marriage and divorce,
names covered with other names.
Mother notices an empty
plate and passes the warm bowl.
The wondering—whose brother, whose second child,
whose husband that remarried so quickly—
feeds out like an anchor line.

Seconds and the dead accumulate.
"Here, this is the last spoonful.
We might as well clean this out."

We empty the bowls, fill the graves.
This is the body.

All Saints' Eve

A Halloween hayride for the church youth
and I can hear them singing now
behind the low-gear chug of the John Deere.
Inside the mask, actually a whole woolly head,
my breathing is a racket that filters their song.
I am to roar and lumber out of darkness.
Here comes the wagon, a raft of Methodist children.
I crouch, big monkey, Darwin's spook,
more man than beast with mischief to prove it.

Their faces contort to fright on cue—
little actors on their rough plank stage.
For an instant the screams are genuine.
Then two elder boys shout, "It's not real"
and jump from the wagon to pursue
their belief. A gorilla in southern hardwood
isn't likely and doubt a good bet.
I rip the awkward suit in three places,
outdistancing their reasoning, wanting only
to leave them dark and fleeting glimpses.
What isn't fully seen is much easier to believe.

V

Sumac

Trash trees,
they grew in gangs
at a useful field's edge.

Lean, scraggly,
they had the look of racket
about them, trees
that would mouth off,
eye your sister
then your mother, trees
like whip handles.
They could take a beating.
Limber, it was hard to break them
and when you did they stank
the way a black snake does,
cornered and touched.

They were bones
with that brown butter marrow
and they didn't break clean.
A hairline fracture
could pinch a blood blister
when you held them.

Nearly straight,
they were our scepters in April
when their tops sprouted
the green buds that leafed out scarlet.
With our jeweled maces
we ruled backyards
and fought too,
jabbing, feinting, whacking,
leaving welts with their quick slaps.
Dark and off to bed,
the pungent musk of kingdom
stayed on our hands.

Dolls

Made babies,
putty skin and hairlines like roots in a riverbank,
toes like dimples in dough.
We dragged them by the hair or one leg,
hugged them, smothered them in our sleep.
Cheap or porcelain,
they could be scolded, told to sit up,
be quiet, quit giggling, act like somebody.

Put down in drawers for naps,
cooed over, cuddled, cried on.
We tested scissors on them.
We left them naked and the dog got at them.
We used allowances
for their wardrobes and gave them dates,
fed them imaginary cakes,
had them slap someone.

Sometimes they died

and were resurrected as an aunt
or woman who raised cattle with her boots on.
Their breasts were surprising
and we wouldn't let boys touch them.

Some were blackened
by getting too close to a fire.
Some would not bend.
Some drank and wet.
Some spoke three words when hugged.
Some had a string to make them talk.
Some had babies of their own.
Some sang.
Even though small, some were tall.
Some came apart.
Some opened their eyes.

Laundry

Like an old song,
the familiar lines repeated,
sheets, shirts, dresses, pants
and, behind, the under things.

Gotten out of again,
grease, the salt of sweat,
the day's slough and smear,
rinsed, wrung, lifted to light.

They wore the wind,
invisible work that like a ballad
hung joy and sorrow
side by each, coming clean.

They waved and walked.
They billowed and snapped,
whispered, waited, sometimes sported
a common beetle like a fancy brooch.

Boots

Caked with manure or mud,
they slouched on doorsteps,
the uppers cracked, sad sacking,
the way the men,

at ease, might lean.
But the shoe part stayed
at attention, toes cocked
as though straining at a lift.

They couldn't go in
where cooking and clean hands
were, where sewing and sheets
were folded and prayers said.

So, they guarded the door,
ready for another day.
Until more work was to be done
they swallowed their tongues.

VI

What They Had to Say

What they had to say
about salt blocks, sparrow hawks, hand brakes,
lace doilies, pieces of fingers the saws dropped,
chopping thistles out of new grass, cash
and carry, nary a pot to piss in, fishing
for flatheads with dead puppies on a trot line,
time and its going-on-ness, messes made
and fell back in, sin and its easy-to-findness,
kindnesses during bad stretches, what fetches
us up from the animal, the handles of hoes
and getting to the end of the furrow and marrow
sucked from the bones to get all the good
should be recorded on gilt-edged scrolls
but won't though they said it
let my record show.

The Last Time He Told It

He loved the story and would tell it
at any gathering where the family in question
or any of their distant kin were mentioned.
"Old man Hillard Taylor, you know he always said
third grade was all the education he needed
for his acreage, had worked his self red-faced
slashing at brush and hacking low limbs
trying to open up the path to the Taylor cabin.
When Ben Simpson came along in his Model T
and asked old Taylor what he was about,
Hillard explained that he had had a letter
from his son away at Fort Wood in the service.
The boy had written that he was 'coming in on a furlough'
and everybody knew they could barely get a mule
up this path." The last time he told it
was at the meal after they buried the Muse boy
sent home from Vietnam in his flag-draped box.
Some few chuckled. Some coughed and all
looked away, out a window and over the fields
as though watching for the foreign words to come.

Archives of The How-It-Was Club

Let's say a Methodist Church basement.
Gathered are the children of an absent-minded God,
themselves absent clear vision, absent the concise hand
needed for captioning the scalloped-edged glimpses
of how they got by, their common history,
quilting, canning, butchering hogs,
that will seem exotic to their children's children
with an assigned interest in local color.

Someone laid hands on a cassette recorder.
They cackle and croon. They sign on,
this is Sallie Murphy, born nineteen hundred and four,
as though these reminiscences are a radio show.
Come on, granny, get to it,
but she's more interested in telling us *who*
than *what* and *what's* what we need
for our current purposes.
This is a different country
and we can't get graded on which cousin
or visitor from Ohio helped prime tobacco.
We need the low-down on gutting a hog.
Wasn't there blood involved?

This is what happens
when you let people tell their own story.
There's no hurry, no precision,
so very little we can use.

Scene Painted on a Two-man Saw Blade

A match to the twin milk crocks
that've been made into lamps,
and the butter churn, lacquered
and buffed bright for a fern to sit,

it rainbows over the knotty pine
mantel, the reds, blues and purples
picking up the colors in the drapes
while rendering, folk-art style,

"the homeplace," which the artist
captured from an old black and white.
The ones who were partner
to that blade's rough buck-and-wing

would lift a sweat-soaked cap
and run a sour bandanna
across their brow. "Now why
you want a thing like that in the house?"

Dollar Bill

Small-town AM station,
morning show,
still doing a gospel number every hour.
Who's listening?
Bacon tenders, baby sitters.
He yucks it up for the insurance office crew,
the stop-in, mini-mart gas shacks.
He's on the counter at The Hub,
talking coffee cups up and down.
A clown, a daily goofball,
regular as sun-up and death,
he reads the obits from the local paper
and sometimes adds a personal note.
Even the disembodied here have an anecdote.
Dashboard and countertop,
new tunes and same old same old,
beer on sale, car tires, paint,
link sausage, the grind and groove
of tune. We're coming up on noon.
Outside, in the parking lot, sparrows bathe
in the dust. Empires rise and fall. He'll notice
and say nothing of it on the air.

Past Due

I'm paying my light bill and need
twelve cents, and I think I feel it
in the pocket of my new
khakis that just this morning
I slid from their mailing pouch
and put on, still cold from their night under the porch light.
What I find
is a slip of paper with the name "Elaine"
typed on it. "That's my mother's name,"
I say to the woman behind
the power company's customer counter.
I'm paying my light bill and need
to forget that my mother's name was waiting
in my new pocket.
"She inspected it," says the power company woman.

I see my mother holding up my pants,
looking them over in the light from a window
because her house, the old homeplace, had no lights
or no inside lights other than what people could carry.
I'm paying my light bill and need
to put away this ticket
that has permitted me to enter the movie
in which my mother is inspecting my pants
before she folds them
and slips her name, which proclaims
the work of her eyes, into the cool pocket.
The house she was born in,
the house with no lights of its own,
is now under the lake,
the lake this company backed up
to hold the power,
the power of water that becomes light,
for which I am, by unspoken agreement, accountable.

Transport in Early Spring

Twin-engine prop jet, Morgantown terminal.
One runway. During rev-up I notice

the dandelions, yellow buttons in spring's
new green. They'll launch later.

Up, we wheel toward Pittsburgh
and buck on the invisible shocks

of carnival air. It's a county fair
ride up here—knocks,

dips and whoop-de-doos. I use
my ticket for a bookmark,

close the box of words
and watch West Virginia slide.

Down there a train makes its way
like a sentence, cars distinct as parts of speech.

It works along a river,
supple for an archaic mode.

Coal, stone, grains and lumber.
Those antique loads could not be lifted.

Locality pulls back on being pulled.
Language only half releases. Its drag is true.

Woodpile

A cure for suburbia,
this short stack of *V*s, *A*s and *O*s.
At least that's the way I read
the butt ends of the logs
snug between two living trees.
It's playing at work,
not like the head high, quartered wedges,
four deep in four racks,
they had to make and hope
a log or two would be left come spring.
They, unread, strong-handed, strong-headed.
Me, one callus on the second finger
where the pen rides, making
my alphabet burn for them.